Earthquakes sometimes crack the ground open

Earthquakes

Aaron Frisch

A⁺
Smart Apple Media

COPYRIGHT

Published by Smart Apple Media

1980 Lookout Drive, North Mankato, MN 56003

Designed by Rita Marshall

Copyright © 2002 Smart Apple Media. International copyright reserved in all countries. No part of this book may be reproduced in any form without written permission from the publisher.

Printed in the United States of America

Photographs by Tom Myers

Library of Congress Cataloging-in-Publication Data

Frisch, Aaron. Earthquakes / by Aaron Frisch. p. cm. — (Natural disasters series)

Includes index.

ISBN 1-58340-123-7

1. Earthquakes—Juvenile literature. [1. Earthquakes.] I. Title. II. Series.

QE521.3 .F75 2001   551.22—dc21   00-052645

First Edition 9 8 7 6 5 4 3 2 1

CONTENTS

What Is an Earthquake?

In 1811 and 1812, the ground in Missouri seemed to come alive. Three different times, the state was rocked by shaking so powerful that some of the ground sank, changing the course of the Mississippi River. These frightening events were earthquakes. An earthquake is a shaking of the ground caused by shifting rock inside the earth. Earthquakes begin deep in the earth. Scientists think that much of the middle of the earth is made up of hot, melted rock called **magma**. The thin,

Earthquakes can let magma rise to the earth's surface

outside layer of the earth is called the crust. The bottom of the crust is made up of huge pieces of rock called plates.

The magma under these plates is always moving. This makes the plates move too. They move very slowly—only about as fast as a person's fingernails grow. Some plates slide toward each other. Other plates slide away from each other. The gap between two plates is called a **fault**. This is where most earthquakes happen. Most faults are deep underground. But some can be seen on the

In 1906, a big earthquake in San Francisco broke many gas lines. This started fires that burned the city for three days.

earth's surface. One of the most famous faults in the world is

the San Andreas Fault. This fault is like a long crack in the

earth. It runs across much of the state of California.

Moving plates can create large cracks in the earth

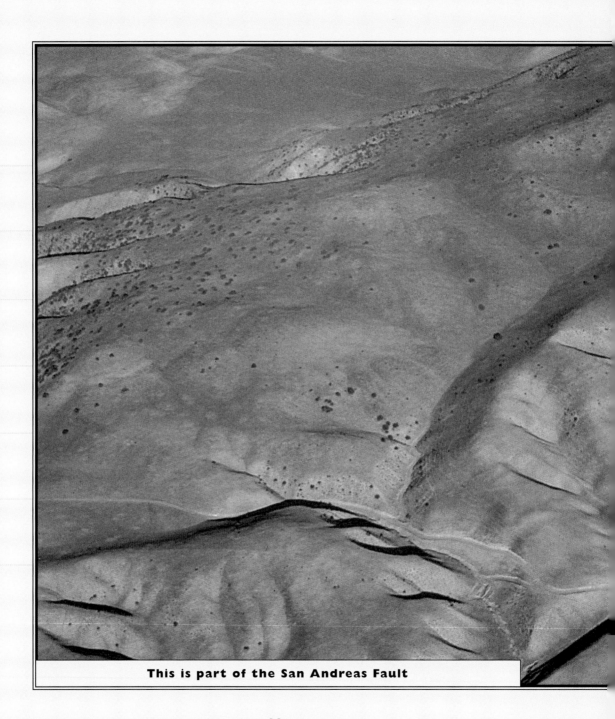

This is part of the San Andreas Fault

How Plates Move

Plates sometimes bump into each other. They push and bend as they try to get past each other. Sometimes one plate may suddenly break or slide up or down. This causes an earthquake. When a plate suddenly moves deep underground, it creates **vibrations** called seismic waves. These waves spread out in all directions. They move through the ground very fast—about four miles (6.4 km) per second. This makes the ground rock back and forth and causes buildings to shake. This shaking may last a few seconds or a few minutes

and during big earthquakes makes a deep rumbling sound.

Earthquakes can cause great damage. Buildings and

bridges often collapse. Fires start when gas lines break. Water

Even concrete can be broken during earthquakes

pipes can burst. Earthquakes that happen under the ocean can create huge waves called **tsunamis**. These waves can be more than 100 feet (30 m) tall and cause terrible flooding wherever they come ashore. Scientists study earthquakes using a device called a seismograph. A seismograph detects underground motion caused by seismic waves. It records the strength of the waves by drawing a series of wavy lines. These lines may be on paper or may be stored in a computer.

In the United States, most earthquakes happen in California. The state with the second-most earthquakes is Alaska.

Measuring Earthquakes

To describe how strong an earthquake is, scientists usually use a measuring system called the **Richter scale**. They

Underwater earthquakes can cause giant waves

use seismographs to measure the ground motion during an earthquake. They then assign the earthquake a number on the scale to indicate how strong it was. The Richter scale was developed in 1935 by a scientist named Charles F. Richter. The scale starts at 1 for weak earthquakes and goes up for stronger ones. Earthquakes measuring 1 or 2 usually can't even be felt. Earthquakes measuring 7 or higher may destroy huge buildings and kill many people. The

During very strong earthquakes, the ground can heave up or down as much as 20 feet (6 m).

Earthquakes can destroy entire cities

biggest earthquake ever recorded was a 9.5 on the Richter

scale. It happened in 1960 in the South American country of

Chile. Luckily, very powerful earthquakes are rare. The earth

has only one severe earthquake every year or two.

Earthquake Precautions

We will never be able to stop earthquakes from

happening. But there are things we can do to protect ourselves.

Scientists watch faults closely and try to predict when an earth-

quake will happen so they can warn people. Engineers design

Buildings in earthquake areas must be strong but flexible

and build stronger buildings in earthquake areas. These build-

ings may have extra-strong walls made of concrete with steel

rods inside. Usually, the safest place to be during an

earthquake is under a table or another **More than**
three million
solid piece of furniture. People who are **people were**
killed by earth-
outside during an earthquake should stay **quakes around**
the world in
away from tall buildings and trees. Even **the 1900s.**

after the shaking stops, people need to be careful. Big earth-

quakes are often followed by many smaller ones called after-

shocks. An earthquake is one of the most powerful

events in nature. Big earthquakes can kill thousands of people

and destroy even large cities. But knowing more about earth-

quakes will help people stay safe when an earthquake happens.

Damage caused by the 1906 earthquake in San Francisco

Make Your Own Seismograph

Seismographs are used to measure how much the ground moves during an earthquake. You can make your own seismograph at home.

What You Need

A large jar with a lid   Tape

A pen   A large roll of paper

What You Do

1. Fill the jar with water and screw the lid on.

2. Put the roll of paper on a table. Then put the jar in the middle of the paper.

3. Use the tape to attach the pen to the jar. The point of the pen should just touch the paper.

4. Grab the end of the paper and pull it toward you slowly (you may need to use one hand to keep the jar in place). The pen should make a straight line.

5. Then ask a friend to shake the table gently while you pull on the paper. The pen should draw small, wavy lines on the paper. These are just like the lines created by a seismograph during an earthquake. The harder the table shakes, the bigger the wavy lines will get.

Major rivers can change paths after an earthquake

Index

Words to Know

fault (FAWLT)—the gap between two plates of rock; it is like a weak spot in the earth's crust

magma (MAG-muh)—hot, melted rock inside the earth

Richter scale (RIK-ter skale)—a system used to measure the strength of an earthquake

seismograph (SIZE-muh-graf)—a device that records shaking movements in the earth

tsunamis (tsoo-NAH-mees)—huge waves caused by earthquakes under the ocean

vibrations (vi-BRAY-shuns)—quick up and down or side to side movements

Read More

Morris, Neil. *Earthquakes.* New York: Crabtree Publishing Company, 1998.

Pope, Joyce. *Earthquakes.* Brookfield, Conn.: Copper Beech Books, 1998.

Sipiera, Paul P. *Earthquakes.* New York: Children's Press, 1998.

Internet Sites

Earthquakes (Canadian Broadcasting Corporation)
http://cbc.ca/news/indepth/earthquake/

National Earthquake Information Center
http://neic.usgs.gov/

United States Geological Survey
http://quake.wr.usgs.gov/

INFORMATION